MW00946567

World of Mammals

Whales

by Scott R. Welvaert

Consultant:
Amy Hellrung
Research Associate
Pacific Whale Foundation
Wailuku, Hawaii

Capstone press

Mankato, Minnesota

Bridgestone Books are published by Capstone Press,
151 Good Counsel Drive, P.O. Box 669, Mankato, Minnesota 56002.
www.capstonepress.com

Library of Congress Cataloging-in-Publication Data
Welvaert, Scott R.
    Whales / by Scott R. Welvaert.
        p. cm.—(Bridgestone books. World of mammals)
    Includes bibliographical references and index.
    ISBN 0-7368-3721-3 (hardcover)
    1. Whales—Juvenile literature. I. Title. II. Series: World of mammals.
QL737.C4W395 2005
599.5—dc22   2004013427

Summary: A brief introduction to whales, discussing their characteristics, habitat, life cycle,
    and predators. Includes a range map, life cycle illustration, and amazing facts.

Editorial Credits
Erika L. Shores, editor; Molly Nei, set designer; Ted Williams, book designer; Erin Scott, Wylde Hare
    Creative, illustrator; Kelly Garvin, photo researcher; Scott Thoms, photo editor

Photo Credits
Bruce Coleman Inc./Masa Ushioda, 6
Francois Gohier, 10
Robin Brandt, 20
Seapics.com/Amos Nachoum, 16; Bob Cranston, 18; James D. Watt, cover; Marilyn & Maris Kazmers, 1;
    Michael S. Nolan, 12; Phillip Colla, 4

1 2 3 4 5 6 10 09 08 07 06 05

Table of Contents

Whales

The biggest animals on earth live in water. Whales are large sea **mammals**. They can be bigger than elephants and taller than giraffes. Like land mammals, whales have backbones and are **warm-blooded**. Unlike land mammals, sea mammals find all of their food in the ocean.

Whales are divided into two groups called toothed whales and **baleen** whales. Toothed whales include dolphins and porpoises. Baleen whales include humpback and blue whales. Baleen whales have no teeth. Their mouths are filled with many thin plates.

◄ The blue whale is the largest animal on earth.

pectoral fins

fluke

What Whales Look Like

Whales have long bodies shaped like rockets. A thick layer of fat under their skin keeps whales warm. The fat is called blubber.

Pectoral fins and a tail help whales swim. The fins are shaped like long flat paddles. The end of their tail is called a **fluke**. Whales move their fluke up and down to swim through water.

Whales have one or two blowholes on top of their heads. Whales breathe air into their lungs through the blowhole.

◄ Like all whales, pilot whales have fins and a fluke to help them swim through the water.

Whales Range Map

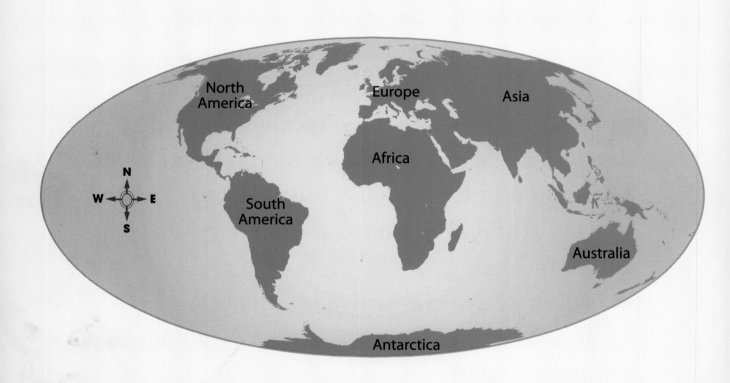

 Where Whales Live

Whales in the World

Whales live in oceans all over the world. Most whales travel in groups called pods or herds. Other whales travel alone.

Many kinds of whales **migrate** in summer and winter. In summer, some whales swim to cold water in the Antarctic or the Arctic to find food. In winter, the whales swim to warm water near the equator. Whales **mate** and give birth in warm water.

◀ Whales live in every ocean in the world.

Whale Habitats

A whale's body is fit to live in its ocean **habitat**. The shape of a whale's body helps it move quickly through the water. Whales cannot see easily underwater, but they can hear very well. They hear sounds from miles away.

Whales must come to the surface of the ocean to breathe. Whales sometimes stick their heads out of the water. When they look around, they are spy-hopping. When whales jump out of the water, they are breaching.

◄ When humpback whales breach, they may be sending messages to other whales.

baleen

What Whales Eat

Toothed whales grasp their food and swallow it whole. Sperm whales dive deep to find squid to eat. Some killer whales swim close to shore to hunt for seals. Other killer whales eat fish.

Baleen whales eat in a different way. They take big gulps of water. Their baleen plates trap small fish and small animals called krill. Baleen whales swallow the fish or krill whole.

◄ A gray whale takes a gulp of water. Its baleen traps krill. The whale then swallows the krill whole.

The Life Cycle of a Whale

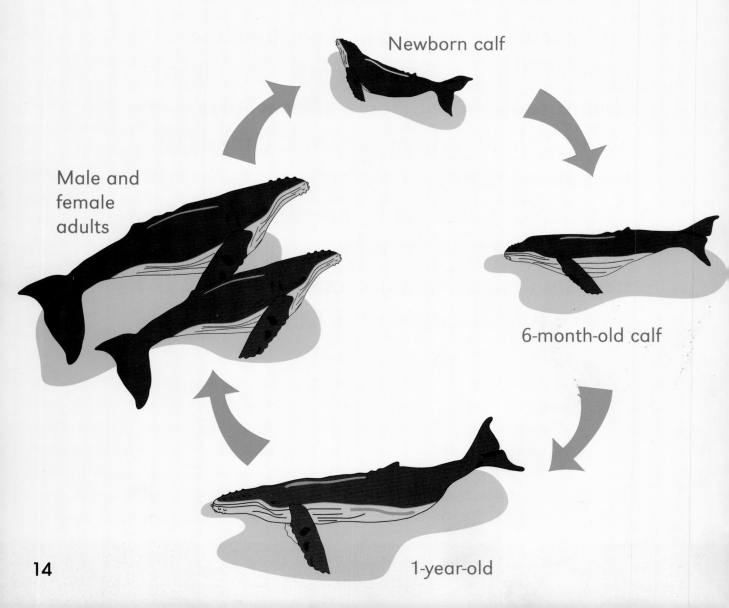

Newborn calf

6-month-old calf

1-year-old

Male and female adults

Producing Young

Whales usually swim to warm areas of the ocean to mate. In the warm ocean water, whales try to attract each other. They try to touch one another. Humpback whales make sounds like songs to attract a mate. Some whales swim in ways that look like a dance.

A female gives birth to a calf about 12 months after mating. The mother pushes its calf to the surface for its first breath of air.

Growing Up

Newborn whale calves are large. A killer whale calf is about 7 feet (2 meters) long at birth. It weighs about 400 pounds (181 kilograms).

For the first year, a whale calf drinks milk from its mother. It then is able to eat fish or krill on its own. Whale calves grow fast. Blue whale calves gain about 200 pounds (91 kilograms) per day until they are full-grown.

◄ A killer whale calf may stay with its mother for its entire life.

Dangers to Whales

Whales have few **predators**. Sharks sometimes attack whales and their calves. Killer whales may attack other whales.

People cause the most harm to whales. Pollution makes ocean water dirty. Chemicals and oil leaks from ships can kill whales. Whales can get sick from eating garbage dumped in the ocean.

Scientists study whales and their habitats. They want to do a better job protecting whales and the places where they live.

◄ Scientists often dive into the ocean to study whales, such as this southern right whale, up close.

Amazing Facts about Whales

- When whales blow air out of their blowholes, water above the blowhole shoots high into the air. These spouts can shoot as high as 30 feet (9 meters).
- Whales make many sounds including chirps, barks, squeaks, and moos. Some scientists think whale sounds can travel as far as 1,000 miles (1,600 kilometers).
- Whales can live to be 90 years old.
- A humpback whale's tongue weighs as much as a pickup truck.

◄ Whales blow air out of their blowholes at speeds of up to 300 miles (483 kilometers) per hour.

Glossary

baleen (buh-LEEN)—a long, thin piece of bonelike material attached to the mouths of some whales; baleen whales trap krill and small fish in their baleen.

fluke (FLOOK)—the wide, flat area at the end of a whale's tail

habitat (HAB-uh-tat)—the place and natural conditions in which an animal lives

mammal (MAM-uhl)—a warm-blooded animal that has a backbone; female mammals feed milk to their young.

mate (MAYT)—to join together to produce young

migrate (MYE-grate)—to move from one area to another

pectoral fin (PEK-tor-uhl FIN)—the hard, flat limb on either side of a whale

predator (PRED-uh-tur)—an animal that hunts other animals for food

warm-blooded (warm-BLUHD-id)—having a body temperature that stays the same

Read More

Laskey, Elizabeth. *Whales.* Sea Creatures. Chicago: Heinemann Library, 2003.

Richardson, Adele D. *Whales: Giants of the Deep.* Wild World of Animals. Mankato, Minn.: Bridgestone Books, 2002.

Internet Sites

FactHound offers a safe, fun way to find Internet sites related to this book. All of the sites on FactHound have been researched by our staff.

Here's how:
1. Visit *www.facthound.com*
2. Type in this special code **0736837213** for age-appropriate sites. Or enter a search word related to this book for a more general search.
3. Click on the **Fetch It** button.

FactHound will fetch the best sites for you!

Index